THE JAR SPELLS

Compendium

Master The Practice of Bottle Spells and Unleash Your Magic.
100 easy Spell Recipes to Manifest Love, Confidence, Prosperity
and much more

Aoife O'Clery

TABLE OF CONTENTS

Chapter 4 : Jar Spells Recipes 31

AUTHOR BIOGRAPHY

❖

Aoife O'Clery is a green witch hailing from County Clare in Ireland, but now resides in London. She comes from a long line of wise women and healers, and has been practising the craft for over 20 years now. She is well-versed in the traditional Irish folk magic and the use of herbs and plants in spellwork.

Growing up in a rural area of Ireland, O'Clery was deeply connected to the land and nature spirits. She spent her childhood exploring the countryside and learning about the plants and animals that lived there. Her love for nature and the magic it holds led to her decision to follow in the footsteps of her ancestors and study witchcraft.

In her twenties, O'Clery moved to London with her partner. She quickly realised that the fast-paced and often hectic nature of urban living required her to work with the energy of the city and adapt her "green witch" spellwork.

Despite the challenges of living in a big city, O'Clery has found a way to keep her connection to the natural world and the magic it holds. She is a firm believer that magic exists in everyday life, from the open fields of County Clare to the smallest apartment of London.

O'Clery's work reflects her passion for Irish tradition, wisdom and folk magic. She has written several books on the subject, and is highly respected in the magic community for her unique perspective on urban magic. Her books are a combination of traditional and modern practices, and a blend of her Irish heritage and her London experiences.

In her books, O'Clery shares her knowledge and experience in a way that is both accessible and practical. She explains how to use traditional practices in an urban setting, and how to incorporate them into modern living. She also provides readers with a variety of spells, rituals, and exercises that can be used to improve their daily lives.

At home in County Clare, O'Clery is a sought-after speaker and teacher, regularly giving workshops and talks on the topic of folk magic. She is passionate about educating others and sharing her knowledge and experience, and is dedicated to helping people connect with their own inner wisdom and power.

Overall, Aoife O'Clery is an accomplished witch, author and teacher. Her unique perspective on urban witchcraft and Irish traditions has helped many people connect with the magic of the natural world, even amidst the hustle and bustle of city life. Her work continues to inspire and empower those who seek to deepen their spiritual practice and live a more magical life.

INTRODUCTION

---❖---

Greetings everyone! I'm Aoife, the author of this book. I grew up in County Clare, Ireland, where I was raised by my magically inclined mother and my even more magically inclined grandmother. They in turn were raised by their witchy mothers and grandmothers, and theirs too. If you can't guess, I come from a long line of wise women and healers.

My grandmother, Oonagh, was a well-known healer in our rural town, attracting many customers who asked her for help. No matter what ailed the person, grandma had a cure. Effortlessly, she was able to use her knowledge of plants and herbs to create potions and tinctures that could alleviate almost any pain and cure any illnesses. She was always seemingly surrounded by people seeking her help, and I was always in awe of her ability to heal and never seem put-out by their constant requests. Her capacity for magic was only trumped by her capacity for kindness.

My most fond memory of my grandmother is from a summer when I was around eight years old when she held my hand and led me out into the garden. We spent hours in the garden that day; her showing me how to identify different plants, and explaining their properties and uses. She told me stories of how she used different herbs to make potions that could alleviate pain and cure illnesses. And then she leant in close, as though she was about to let me in on a very special secret…

"Given enough time, the body will heal itself," she explained, "if you *really* want to help people, use these plants to heal their hearts, not their bodies."

I didn't realise it at the time, but she was introducing me to magic.

As the years went on, my grandmother started to teach me simple spells and charms that I could use to help my friends and family. I remember feeling so excited and proud when I was able to use my newfound knowledge to help my cousin find the courage to swim without armbands, or heal my best friend's disappointment after a poor grade in an exam.

Although I was lucky to grow up in a family and live in a community where witchcraft was openly accepted, I never thought I would follow in my mother and grandmother's footsteps. Being a "real witch" wasn't something that interested me. It wasn't until my late teens that I realised I had a special knack for magic (a story for another book) and I began to experiment with different spells and potions. Word spread across County Clare that I was quite talented, and soon I became as sought after as my grandmother before me.

Years later, when my grandmother passed away, people flocked to me asking for my help. I knew then that I had a responsibility to share my gift with others. I started to teach people about folk magic through workshops and talks, and of course, I thought about writing a book.

My grandmother was a wise and kind woman, and I will always be grateful for the time she spent teaching me about magic. She instilled in me a deep respect for the power of plants and nature, and taught me how to use them to bring healing and happiness to others. Her lessons stayed with me throughout my life.

I've thought about her a lot in writing this book, and even more since giving birth to a baby girl of my own…

As a mother of a newborn baby girl, I am filled with a sense of wonder and amazement at the miracle of life. Holding my daughter in my arms, I am reminded of the magic that surrounds us every day and I feel a deep sense of responsibility to pass on the knowledge and traditions of magic to the next generation.

Just like my grandmother did with me, I want to introduce my daughter to the magic of plants and herbs from a young age. I want to teach her how to identify different plants, and explain their properties and uses. I want to take her on walks in nature and show her how to collect different herbs and flowers for spells and potions. I want her to understand the power of the natural world and how we can use it to bring healing and happiness to ourselves and others.

As my daughter grows up, I also want to teach her the importance of intention and visualisation in spell work. I want her to understand the power of her thoughts and emotions, and how they can be used to create change in her life. I want her to learn how to set intentions, visualise her desires, and how to use jar spells as a tool for manifestation. I want her to understand the importance of self-care and self-reflection in the practice of magic, and how to approach jar spells with a sense of balance and self-awareness.

As a mother and a witch, I am excited to share my love and knowledge of magic with my daughter. I am looking forward to watching her grow and develop her own unique relationship with the natural world, and to watching her use magic to bring positive change in her life and the lives of others. I am confident that by passing on the traditions and teachings of magic, I am not only preserving an ancient practice but also empowering the next generation to create the world they want to live in.

It was these thoughts, of my grandmother, my daughter, and teaching others about magic, that inspired me to write this book.

After my grandmother had died, my partner and I moved to London in England. Moving from a very rural landscape to a capital city was a difficult transition and I realised that practising witchcraft in an urban environment was very different from what I had been used to. No longer could I practise openly, and sourcing ingredients became far more difficult. This was when the inspiration for my book hit me. I would share my traditional Irish witchcraft and how to adapt it for an urban setting. But what would that look like? … Jar spells!

One of the most significant advantages of jar spells is that they can be made and used discreetly. They can be hidden easily, worn as jewellery, or used as decoration in the home. This makes them an ideal choice for those who are not able to practise magic openly. Jar spells allow individuals to create magic in a way that is private and personal, allowing them to connect with the spiritual realm in a way that feels safe and comfortable for them.

Jar spells are also great for those living in rural or urban environments. Despite what other jar spell books may say; you can swap out the ingredients you don't have, for the ones you do, and it won't affect the intention. This is all possible using something called "magic correspondence"; something I go into later in the book. But this means that no matter where you live, you can create spells that are tailored to your specific needs and intentions.

In addition to the practical aspects of jar spells, I also touch on the psychological and spiritual aspects of the practice. I discuss the power of intention and visualisation, and how they can be used to enhance the effectiveness of jar spells.

Whether you are new to jar spells or an experienced practitioner, this book will provide you with the knowledge and inspiration you need to create your own jar spells and harness the power of this ancient practice, regardless of where you live. The book will guide you through the process of adapting your practice to an urban environment and provide you with tips and tricks for performing magic discreetly.

I hope that my book will inspire you to explore the world of jar spells and discover the power of this ancient practice for yourself. It is my wish that this book will empower you to connect with the natural world, tap into the energy of the city, and create magic in a way that feels safe and comfortable for you.

CHAPTER I

❖

THE HISTORY OF JAR SPELLS

Jar spells, sometimes known as bottle spells or container spells, are a form of folk magic that involves using a sealed container, typically a jar or bottle, to trap and contain a specific energy or intention. The basic principle behind jar spells is that by physically containing an intention or energy, the spell is given a physical form that can be easily stored and maintained. This makes jar spells an easy and convenient way to practise magic, as well as a powerful tool for achieving specific goals.

Folk magic is a term that refers to the traditional, often unofficial, magical practices of a particular culture or community. It encompasses a wide range of beliefs and practices, including spells, charms, divination, and other forms of magic that are passed down through generations. Folk magic uses the tools and ingredients available to the practitioner; nothing particularly hard to find or ceremonial.

Folk magic is often deeply rooted in the cultural beliefs and traditions of a particular community, and it is often used to address everyday problems and concerns. The folk magic and jar spells in this book are taken from the traditions I have learnt as an Irish witch, but there are plenty of other cultures and countries that have their own take on jar spells.

In the Republic of Ireland and the United Kingdom, folk magic has a rich history dating back to ancient times. The Celts, who inhabited these islands before the arrival of the Romans, had a complex belief system that included a wide range of magical practices. These practices included the use of charms, spells, and divination to bring about desired outcomes and to protect against harm. In fact, jar spells weren't just used by witches and healers; they were used by the regular folk too. In the UK, there is a particular type of jar spell called a "witch bottle" that was used as a form of protection against witches and other malicious spirits.

In contemporary and traditional witchcraft, jar spells can be used for a wide variety of purposes; love spells, protection spells, and spells to bring about prosperity or good luck. Jar spells can also be used for more specific goals, such as healing, banishing negative energy, or manifesting a particular desire. One of the main benefits of jar spells is that they can be easily customised to suit the specific needs and intentions of the practitioner.

When creating a jar spell, it's important to choose the right ingredients and items that are symbolic of your desired outcome. It's also important to choose the right type of jar or container, as well as the right lid or seal to ensure that the energy and intention are contained within the jar. Some practitioners prefer to use specific colours or shapes of jars, while others prefer to use natural materials such as clay or glass.

Jar spells can be as simple or as complex as the practitioner desires, but the key is to choose ingredients and items that are symbolic of the desired outcome. For example, a spell for protection might include items such as garlic, salt, and iron nails, while a spell for love might include rose petals, cinnamon, and a personal item such as a photo of the person you wish to attract.

You will notice that many of the jar spells in this book are often used in conjunction with other forms of magic, such as candle magic, herbal magic, and crystal magic. This allows the practitioner to create a powerful and synergistic spell that combines the energies of different magical elements. For example, a spell to manifest financial abundance might include a jar filled with items such as cinnamon, pyrite, and a green candle, all of which are associated with wealth and abundance.

Once the jar spell is created, it's important to properly charge and activate it. This can be done through visualisation, meditation, or by reciting specific words or phrases. The jar spell can then be placed in a special location where it can be easily accessed and maintained. Some practitioners prefer to hide their jar spells, while others prefer to keep them on display in a specific location such as an altar or windowsill.

It's important to keep in mind that jar spells are a form of magic, and should be treated with respect and care. Always consider the ethics of your spellwork and the potential consequences of your actions. I won't dissuade you from using a jar spell for negative or harmful purposes, but instead I will remind you to consider other options first.

In conclusion, jar spells are a versatile and powerful form of folk magic that have a rich history in Ireland and the UK. They can be used for a wide variety of purposes, and can be easily customised to suit the specific needs and intentions of the practitioner. Whether you are an experienced practitioner or new to the world of magic, jar spells can be a great way to add a touch of magic to your life.

CHAPTER 2

PREPARATION AND ADVICE

Choosing a Jar

When choosing a jar or container for a jar spell, consider the following factors:

Material: Glass is a common choice for jar spells because it is transparent and allows you to see the contents of the jar. Depending on the spell, you may need a jar that can withstand high temperatures or be frozen without breaking. This is important to consider if the spell involves lighting candles or using a flame, or if the spell calls for freezing the contents of the jar. Make sure that the jar you choose is safe to use in the specific conditions required by your spell.

Size: The size of the jar should be appropriate for the spell you are doing. A small jar may be sufficient for a simple spell, while a larger jar may be needed for a spell with more ingredients.

Seal: The jar should have a well-fitting lid to keep the contents contained.

Symbolic meaning: You may wish to choose a container that has a symbolic meaning. For example, a jar made of red glass could be used for a spell related to love or passion.

Discretion: You may want to keep your jar spells private and not want others to know that you are doing magic. Consider choosing a jar or container that is not easily recognisable as a magical tool, such as a plain or everyday looking jar, to maintain discretion.

Cleansing the Space and Supplies

Cleansing your space and supplies before making jar spells is an important step in the spell-casting process. This helps to ensure that the energy surrounding the space and materials is positive and free from any negative influences. Unless stated otherwise, all jar spells start with a cleansing process.

The three most common ways of cleansing your space and supplies are:

Sound: Cleansing with sound can be done by singing, chanting, playing musical instruments, or using singing bowls, bells, and cymbals.

Smoke: Cleansing with smoke can be done by burning herbs such as garden sage, bay leaves or burning incense. This is the method I suggest. To smoke cleanse; light an incense stick and waft the smoke across your ingredients, supplies and around the room. Before filling the jar, put the tip of the incense inside the container so it fills with smoke. While you continue the spell, let the incense burn down naturally.

Oil: Cleansing with oil can be done by anointing objects or yourself (assuming it's skin safe) with specially prepared oil.

IMPORTANT: I do not suggest cleansing with water. Some gemstones like malachite and hematite may create toxic fumes when they come in contact with water! Always research the properties of the materials you plan to use and take necessary precautions to protect yourself.

Intention and Visualisation

Many of the spells in this book will require you to write an "intention" on a slip of paper, which in turn is placed inside the jar.

An intention means deciding what you want to accomplish with the spell and what energy you want to bring into/expel from your life. Sometimes an intention will be a whole sentence, but sometimes it can just be a word, name, initial or symbol.

Not all recipes in this book will call for a written intention; but many people find it to be a useful step in the adaptation of and creation of their own spells as it helps to focus their mind and energy.

After making your jar spell, I also suggest holding the jar in your hands and visualising the intention being made true. This is called "manifestation"; the process by which your energy makes the magic realised. Again, not all spells will call for a visualisation, but many find it useful.

Disposal and Reusing Supplies

There are a few ways to determine when a jar spell is ready to be disposed of. One method is to set a specific time frame for the spell to work, such as one week, one month, or one year. Once that time has passed, the spell is considered to have run its course and can be disposed of.

Another way to determine when a jar spell is ready to be disposed of is to observe the contents of the jar. If the ingredients have dried up, changed colour, or otherwise altered in appearance, it may be a sign that the spell has reached completion.

Here are two ways to dispose of your jar spell:
1. Throw the jar into fast running water. This is a traditional method that has been used for centuries, but it's fallen out of favour in the last two decades. With a planet and nature suffering from pollution and growing landfills, throwing your jar and its contents into a river hardly seems appropriate anymore. Instead I'd suggest the second method.
2. Open the jar and remove the items. Dispose of any ingredients that have decomposed or can not be salvaged. Clean the jar and any ingredients that can be reused. Be sure to cleanse with smoke or sound before reusing these items in a future jar spell.

Reversing a Jar Spell

To reverse a jar spell, follow the instructions in the previous section regarding disposal. In addition to this, as you remove the ingredients, make sure to visualise the spell no longer having an effect. You may wish to repeat a simple mantra such as "undo, reverse, no more it shall be".

Magic Water

Many spells in this book will require the use of magic water; specifically moon water, sun water, or storm water.

Magic water, also known as charged water, is water that has been infused with the energy of natural elements such as the moon, sun, or storms. The process of creating magic water involves exposing a container of water to the energy of the chosen element, such as leaving it outside during a full moon or a sunny day. Some practitioners also choose to include a clear quartz gemstone in the container to amplify the energy. Once the water has been charged, it can be stored in a cool, dark place and used for various purposes.

Moon water, for example, is believed to be particularly useful for rituals and spells related to intuition, emotions, and femininity. It can be used to anoint candles, as a substitute for holy water in rituals, or added to a bath for a moon-blessing ritual. Sun water, on the other hand, is believed to be useful for rituals and spells related to vitality, creativity, and masculinity. It can be used to anoint candles, added to a bath for a sun-blessing ritual or added to a spray bottle for a DIY room and body spray. Storm water is believed to be useful for rituals and spells related to change, power and protection. It can be used to anoint candles, added to a bath for a storm-blessing ritual, or used to cleanse and purify objects or spaces.

Moon water is water that has been charged by the energy of the moon. To make moon water, you will need:
- A glass or ceramic container with a lid.
- Spring, purified, or tap water.
- A clear quartz crystal (optional).

Instructions:
1. Fill your container with water.
2. Place the container outside during a full moon, or in a location where it will be exposed to the moonlight.
3. Leave the container outside for at least 4 hours, or overnight if possible.
4. Optionally, you can place a clear quartz gemstone in the container to amplify the energy of the moon.
5. Bring the container inside and store in a cool, dark place.

Sun water is water that has been charged by the energy of the sun. To make sun water, you will need:
- A glass or ceramic container with a lid.
- Spring, purified, or tap water.
- A clear quartz crystal (optional).

Instructions:

1. Fill your container with water.
2. Place the container outside during a sunny day, or in a location where it will be exposed to sunlight.
3. Leave the container outside for at least 1-2 hours, or for as long as you would like depending on your desired strength.
4. Optionally, you can place a clear quartz gemstone in the container to amplify the energy of the sun.
5. Bring the container inside and store in a cool, dark place.

Storm water is water that has been collected during a storm and charged by the storm's energy. To make storm water, you will need:
- A glass or ceramic container with a lid.
- A day or night when it is going to rain or there is going to be a storm.
- A clear quartz crystal (optional).

Instructions:
1. Place the container outside during a storm.
2. Leave the container outside for the duration of the storm.
3. Optionally, you can place a clear quartz gemstone in the container to amplify the energy of the storm.
4. Bring the container inside and store in a cool, dark place.

Magic Salt

Many spells in this book will require the use of salt; specifically white salt, black salt, pink salt, or green salt.

White salt is nothing more than good old regular table salt.

Pink salt is Himalayan pink salt; although, if you do not have any, white salt is a fine substitute.

Black salt, also known as "witch's salt," is a common ingredient used in various forms of witchcraft. It is believed to provide protection and is often used as a barrier against negative energy. Here is a simple recipe for making black salt:

Ingredients:
- White table salt.

- Ash left over from burnt incense.

Instructions:
1. Mix the white salt and ash together.
2. Keep the black salt in an airtight container.

Green salt, also known as "herb salt," is a type of salt that is infused with herbs and is often used in magic and witchcraft for its believed healing and protective properties. Here is a simple recipe for making green salt:

Ingredients:
- White table salt.
- Rosemary.
- Sage.
- Mint.
- Basil.

Instructions:
1. Grind the dried herbs in a food processor or with a mortar and pestle until they are a fine powder.
2. Mix the salt and herb powder together in a bowl.
3. Spread the mixture out on a baking sheet and place it in a warm, dry place to dry for at least 24 hours.
4. Once the salt is dry, store it in an airtight container.

CHAPTER 3

MAGICAL CORRESPONDENCES:

MAKING AND ADAPTING YOUR OWN JAR SPELLS

ncluded in this book are 100 jar spell recipes, but what if you don't have all the ingredients required? Will a spell still work if you swap out one ingredient for another? Will it still work if you forget to add something? Can you alter the recipes to make your own spells? These are all common questions, and I'm here to tell you that creating your own jar spell recipe is actually very easy. And yes, you can swap out ingredients if needed. All you need are the correspondences.

"Magical correspondence" is the belief that certain objects, symbols, or elements have a symbolic or spiritual connection to one another. It is this connection that enables us to replace one ingredient or another, without any repercussion, because they are energetically connected.

Additionally; moon phases, days of the weeks, certain times of the year also correspond to various colours, symbols, plants, etc. This means that you can increase the potency of your jar spells by choosing to create it at specific times.

Below you will find a series of correspondence tables I have created especially for the book; there is a table for each category of spell (protection, good fortune/luck, money, confidence, career, self-improvement, relationships, home, metaphysics and magic, and hexes). All you need to do is find the table that matches your spell-type, and choose alternative supplies from the list.

Example 1: Lucy wants to make the "Self Love Spell" but she is missing hibiscus and rosehip. She goes to the correspondence table entitled "Love and Relationship Correspondence" and chooses new supplies that she already has.

The next examples show you how to use the tables to create your jar spells from scratch.

Example 2: Joseph wants to make a jar spell to protect his daughter from bullies. He turns to the table entitled "Protection Correspondence" and chooses between three to five items he has at home. He decides he will also add an intention written on a slip of paper.

Example 3: Ramona wants to make a jar spell that encourages good fortune. She turns to the table entitled "Good Fortune and Luck Correspondence" and chooses between three and five items she has at home. She also checks the "Moon Phase" section within that table to find out which moon phase will work best for her spell and increase its potency.

BEGINNER TIP: The spell needs rose petals but you only have rose oil? The spell asks for blackberry leaves but you only have blackberry jam? Or the spell asks for lemon peel but you only have lemon juice? No problem! It's all about the correspondence and the energy, not the physical form of the ingredient. It's very common for witches to swap out peppermint leaves for peppermint tea. Use what you have to hand!

ADVANCED TIP: Just because your spell is for protection, doesn't mean you have to choose items ONLY from the "Protection Correspondence Table". If you need protection from someone who has physically hurt you, it might be beneficial to add items from the "Confidence Correspondence Table" and items from the "Hex Correspondence Table". This mixing-and-matching approach can be used for any type of jar spell.

PROTECTION CORRESPONDENCE

HERBS AND PLANTS
Agrimony, Aloe, Amaranth, Anemone, Angelica, Asafoetida, Basil, Bamboo, Black Cohosh, Blackberry, Bloodroot, Burdock, Broom, Carnation, Cinquefoil, Cinnamon, Clove, Coltsfoot, Comfrey, Coriander, Cowslip, Cumin, Daisy, Dandelion, Dill, Fennel, Fern, Feverfew, Flax, Foxglove, Geranium, Ginseng, Heather, Honeysuckle, Ivy, Jasmine, Lavender, Lilac, Lily, Mandrake, Marjoram, Monkshood, Mustard, Orris Root, Pennyroyal, Peony, Pepper, Periwinkle, Primrose, Raspberry, Reed, Rue, Sandalwood, Snapdragon, Spearmint, Sweet Woodruff, Thyme, Thistle, Valerian, Vervain, Violet, Water Lily, Wormwood, Yarrow.

MOON PHASE
New, Waxing, Full.

DAY OF THE WEEK
Monday, Saturday, Sunday.

GEMSTONES
Agate, Amber, Amethyst, Angelite, Aquamarine, Aventurine, Calcite, Carnelian, Cat's Eye, Citrine, Diamond, Emerald, Garnet, Hematite, Jade, Jasper, Jet, Kunzite, Lepidolite, Malachite, Obsidian, Onyx, Peridot, Petrified Wood, Pyrite, Quartz, Rose Quartz, Ruby, Sunstone, Tanzanite, Tiger's Eye, Topaz, Tourmaline, Turquoise, Zircon.

WHEEL OF THE YEAR
Litha.

COLOURS
Black, Blue, Brown, Gold, Green, Purple, Red, Silver, White, Yellow.

GOOD FORTUNE AND LUCK CORRESPONDENCE

HERBS AND PLANTS	MOON PHASE
Allspice, Basil, Bergamot, Blackberry, Bluebell, Broom, Chamomile, Cinnamon, Cinquefoil, Clove, Clover, Comfrey, Cowslip, Cumin, Dill, Fern, Flax, Grape, Ginger, Heliotrope, Honeysuckle, Iris, Jasmine, Mandrake, Marjoram, Mistletoe, Myrrh, Nutmeg, Peony, Periwinkle, Patchouli, Poppy, Sage, Saffron, Snapdragon, St. John's Wort, Vervain.	Full.
	DAY OF THE WEEK Thursday, Sunday.
GEMSTONES	**WHEEL OF THE YEAR**
Agate, Aventurine, Bloodstone, Calcite, Citrine, Jade, Jasper, Lodestone, Malachite, Opal, Peridot, Quartz, Pyrite, Ruby, Sapphire, Tiger's Eye, Topaz, Tourmaline, Turquoise, Zircon.	Ostara, Beltane.
	COLOURS Blue, Gold, Green.

MONEY AND WEALTH CORRESPONDENCE

HERBS AND PLANTS	MOON PHASE
Anise, Basil, Bergamot, Blackberry, Chamomile, Cinnamon, Cinquefoil, Clover, Comfrey, Cowslip, Dandelion, Dill, Fennel, Fern, Flax, Gardenia, Grape, Heliotrope, Honeysuckle, Iris, Lemon Balm, Mandrake, Marjoram, Mustard, Nutmeg, Patchouli, Peppermint, Periwinkle, Poppy, Sage, Saffron, St. John's Wort, Snapdragon, Spearmint, Sunflower, Sweet Woodruff, Thyme, Valerian, Vervain.	Full, Waxing.
	DAY OF THE WEEK Thursday, Wednesday, Saturday, Sunday.
GEMSTONES	**WHEEL OF THE YEAR**
Agate, Amazonite, Aventurine, Bloodstone, Calcite, Emerald, Jade, Jasper, Malachite, Moss Agate, Opal, Peridot, Pyrite, Sapphire, Staurolite, Topaz, Tourmaline, Zircon.	Mabon.
	COLOURS Brown, Copper, Gold, Green, Orange, Silver.

CONFIDENCE CORRESPONDENCE

HERBS AND PLANTS	MOON PHASE
Basil, Bergamot, Cardamom, Carnation, Fern, Geranium, Heather, Honeysuckle, Nettle, Passionflower, Reed, Rose, Rosemary, Thistle, Thyme, Yarrow.	Full, Waxing.
	DAY OF THE WEEK Sunday.
GEMSTONES Agate, Aragonite, Aventurine, Bloodstone, Blue Lace Agate, Calcite, Carnelian, Citrine, Diamond, Garnet, Hematite, Jade, Labradorite, Larimar, Moss Agate, Obsidian, Onyx, Opal, Rhodonite, Rose Quartz, Tiger's Eye, Tourmaline, Zircon, Zoisite.	**WHEEL OF THE YEAR** Litha.
	COLOURS Blue, Gold, Orange.

WORK AND CAREER CORRESPONDENCE

HERBS AND PLANTS	MOON PHASE
Allspice, Basil, Bamboo, Borage, Cinnamon, Frankincense, Lemon Balm, Lilac, Marigold, Mistletoe, Patchouli, Peony, Sage.	Full, Waxing.
	DAY OF THE WEEK Thursday, Wednesday, Saturday.
GEMSTONES Bloodstone, Emerald, Jade, Lodestone, Malachite, Tourmaline.	**WHEEL OF THE YEAR** Imbolc.
	COLOURS Blue, Green, Orange.

SELF IMPROVEMENT CORRESPONDENCE	
HERBS AND PLANTS Blackberry, Chamomile, Clover, Lavender, Myrrh, Patchouli, Sage, Sandalwood, Vervain, Water Lily.	**MOON PHASE** Mabon.
	DAY OF THE WEEK Any.
GEMSTONES Agate, Amazonite, Amethyst, Aragonite, Blue Lace Agate, Calcite, Fluorite, Garnet, Hematite, Jade, Jasper, Jet, Kunzite, Lodestone, Malachite, Obsidian, Onyx, Peridot, Smoky Quartz, Staurolite, Tiger's Eye, Tourmaline, Turquoise, Zircon.	**WHEEL OF THE YEAR** Mabon.
	COLOURS Black, Brown, Green, White, Yellow.

LOVE AND RELATIONSHIP CORRESPONDENCE	
HERBS AND PLANTS Aloe, Anise, Basil, Burdock, Carnation, Cardamom, Chrysanthemum, Cinquefoil, Cumin, Daffodil, Daisy, Dill, Fern, Feverfew, Frankincense, Ginger, Heather, Heliotrope, Honeysuckle, Iris, Ivy, Lilac, Marigold, Marjoram, Mugwort, Moonwort, Mullein, Mustard, Myrrh, Nutmeg, Periwinkle, Poppy, Rose, Sage, Saffron, Sandalwood, Skullcap, Spikenard, Spearmint, Thyme, Valerian, Violet, Water Lily, Yarrow, Wormwood.	**MOON PHASE** Full, Waxing.
	DAY OF THE WEEK Monday, Friday.
GEMSTONES Agate, Alexandrite, Amazonite, Amethyst, Aventurine, Bloodstone, Calcite, Diamond, Diopside, Emerald, Garnet, Jasper, Lepidolite, Lodestone, Malachite, Rhodochrosite, Sapphire, Sardonyx, Tanzanite, Tourmaline, Tsavorite, Turquoise, Zoisite.	**WHEEL OF THE YEAR** Ostara.
	COLOURS Green, Pink, Red, White.

HOUSE AND HOME CORRESPONDENCE

HERBS AND PLANTS	MOON PHASE
Angelica, Basil, Bergamot, Black Cohosh, Bluebell, Burdock, Carnation, Chamomile, Comfrey, Corn, Geranium, Frankincense, Honeysuckle, Ivy, Lilac, Meadowsweet, Mullein, Myrrh, Patchouli, Primrose, Sage, Sandalwood, Spikenard, Sunflower, Sweet Woodruff, Vervain, Yarrow.	New, Full, Waxing.
	DAY OF THE WEEK Any.
GEMSTONES	**WHEEL OF THE YEAR**
Agate, Alexandrite, Amazonite, Amber, Amethyst, Andalusite, Aragonite, Aventurine, Citrine, Fluorite, Garnet, Hematite, Jasper, Lepidolite, Lodestone, Obsidian, Onyx, Peridot, Quartz, Rhodonite, Serpentine, Smoky Quartz, Sodalite, Staurolite, Tiger's Eye, Tourmaline, Turquoise.	Mabon, Ostara.
	COLOURS Brown, Gray, Green, Purple, Orange, Pink, White.

METAPHYSICS AND MAGIC CORRESPONDENCE

HERBS AND PLANTS	MOON PHASE
Alder, Apple, Blackthorn, Bodhi, Carnation, Cinnamon, Cinquefoil, Elder, Frankincense, Garlic, Goldenseal, Ginseng, Ginger, Hawthorn, Hazel, Laurel, Mandrake, Mugwort, Mushroom, Mullein, Mistletoe, Nettle, Palm, Peony, Patchouli, Rosemary, Rue, Sage, Sandalwood, St. John's Wort, Sunflower, Vanilla, Vervain, Willow, Rowan.	New, Full.
	DAY OF THE WEEK Monday, Friday.
GEMSTONES	**WHEEL OF THE YEAR**
Amber, Diamond, Jet, Labradorite, Lodestone, Obsidian, Sapphire, Staurolite, Tanzanite.	Samhain.
	COLOURS Black.

HEX CORRESPONDENCE

HERBS AND PLANTS	MOON PHASE
Agrimony, Angelica, Asafoetida, Basil, Betony, Broom, Clove, Clover, Comfrey, Cumin, Fern, Frankincense, Garlic, Galangal, Heliotrope, Horehound, Lilac, Mandrake, Mistletoe, Mugwort, Mullein, Myrrh, Nettle, Peony, Pepper, Peppermint, Patchouli, Rose, Rosemary, Rue, Sandalwood, St. John's Wort, Snapdragon, Star Anise, Thistle, Vervain, Violet, Wormwood, Yarrow.	Waning, New.
	DAY OF THE WEEK Saturday.
GEMSTONES Aquamarine, Aventurine, Beryl, Bloodstone, Chrysoprase, Jasper, Rhodonite.	**WHEEL OF THE YEAR** Imbolc.
	COLOURS Black, Green, Purple.

CHAPTER 4

JAR SPELLS RECIPES

Protection Jar Spells

---❖---

A Simple Protection Spell

This protection spell is perfect for beginners. Remember; simple does not mean ineffective! Sometimes the most obvious and simple spells work the best.

Supplies
- Jar or container.
- Paper.
- Pen.
- White salt.
- Black candle.

Instructions:
1. Take a slip of paper, write your name three times.
2. Turn the paper by 90 degrees and write the following statement over the top of your name: "I am protected by the divine, I am protected by the divine, I am protected by the divine."
3. Fold the paper towards you, with the intention of attracting protection.
4. Continue to fold the paper as many times as you need.
5. Place the paper in the jar.
6. Add white salt.
7. Close the jar and hold it in your hands.
8. Focus on sending your energy into the jar.
9. Seal the top of the jar with wax.

Freezer Spell

This spell is designed to protect you from unwanted people in your life by "putting them on ice". Rather than attracting protection, it is pushing the unwanted person away. Leave this spell in the freezer for one to three moon cycles, after which you let the ice thaw naturally and dispose of the contents.

Supplies
- A freezer-safe jar or container.
- Paper.
- Pen.
- Water.

Instructions:
1. Take a slip of paper and write the first name and surname of the person you wish to dispel from your life. If it is unsafe to use their name, consider using initials, a code, or a symbol.
2. Fold the paper in half, away from yourself, with the intention of pushing that person away from you.
3. Fold the paper as many times as you need.
4. Place the paper in the jar.
5. Add a small amount of water to the jar, leaving room for the water to expand when it's frozen.
6. Close the jar.
7. Put the jar in the freezer.

Protected and Blessed Spell

A jar spell to keep you safe and bring forth blessings.

Supplies
- A jar or container.
- White salt.
- Garlic.
- Pepper.
- Lemon juice.
- Nasturtium flower or calendula flower.
- Amber gemstone.
- Paper.
- Pen.
- A black or yellow candle.

Instructions:
1. Add the ingredients to the jar.
2. On a slip of paper write the following mantra; "I am protected. I am safe. I am blessed."

3. Add the paper to the jar and close the lid.
4. Seal the jar with wax.

Black Candle Protection Spell

A jar spell for a longer lasting protection. This is best performed on a waxing moon phase.

Supplies
- A jar or container.
- Nutmeg.
- Garlic.
- Cinnamon.
- Coconut.
- Rosemary.
- Rose petals.
- Frankincense or lemongrass incense.
- Carnelian gemstone.
- Citrine gemstone.
- Malachite gemstone.
- Black candle.
- A pin/needle.

Instructions:
1. Take the pin/needle and scrape into the wax of the unlit candle. Write one or two words to describe from what you need protecting. That could be a name, initials, or a symbol that means something to you.
2. Light the candle and let it burn whilst you fill the jar with ingredients.
3. Close the lid of the jar.
4. Drip some wax onto the lid of the jar and stick the candle to it.
5. Let the wax drip down until it burns itself out.
6. Bury the jar under a tree.

Protection Charm Spell

This protection spell requires a little preparation; you will need a "charm" that is carried around on your person for a week before starting the spell. The charm can be as simple as a coin, gemstone, pebble, an odd sock you no longer need, or something else. Just make sure to keep it on your person for a week leading up to making the jar.

Supplies
- A jar or container.
- Bay leaf.
- Black pepper.
- Sage.
- Cloves.
- White salt.
- Black tourmaline gemstone.
- Homemade charm.
- Black candle.

Instructions:
1. Add the ingredients to the jar.
2. Add the homemade charm.
3. Close the jar and seal with black wax.

New Year Protection Spell

This spell is best performed on the first full moon of January, and will encourage protective energies.

Supplies
- A jar or container.
- Rose petals.
- Cinnamon.
- Clove.
- Obsidian.
- A black, white, gold, or silver candle.

Instructions:
1. Facing south, lay your ingredients and jar in front of you.
2. One by one, hold the ingredients in your hands, and hold them to the sky for nine seconds before placing them in the jar.
3. Close the jar and seal with candle wax.

Persephone Protection Spell

This jar spell calls on the deity of Persephone. It's ok if you do not believe in deities, or if Persephone is not one of the deities with whom you usually work. This spell is about using the energy of the mythology to create protection.

Persephone is a deity from the Greek pantheon, kidnapped by Hades, the god of the underworld. Eventually she makes a bargain with Hades in which she spends winter with him in the underworld, and summers in the land of the living; moving between the two with ease and grace.

Supplies
- A jar or container.
- Basil.
- Pomegranate seeds.
- Cherry seeds or cherry blossoms.
- White salt.
- A black, red, purple or white candle.

Instructions:
1. Before starting the jar spell, take a few moments to meditate on the story of Persephone. Think about her resilience and ability to move through the realms. Ask her for protection as you move through your life; through the good and bad.
2. Add the ingredients to the jar.
3. Close the jar and seal with wax.

The Other Folk Protection Spell

People from all across the world believe in the Other Folk and their power. I grew up knowing them as "little people" or "wee folk", but different cultures know them by different names. In this jar spell we call upon their energy to protect us.

Supplies
- A jar or container.
- White salt.
- Sugar or syrup.
- Jam.
- Bread.

- Rose petals.
- Thyme.
- Paper.
- Pen.
- A black, purple or white candle.

Instructions:
1. Add the white salt, rose petals, and thyme to the jar.
2. Add a small amount of sugar, or syrup to the jar.
3. On a slip of paper write the following plea; "I ask for your protection and in return I will make an offering."
4. Place the paper in the jar.
5. Close the lid and seal with wax.
6. When the evening comes, leave a small portion of jam on bread outside as an offering to the Other Folk.

Tree Protection Spell

Trees are often overlooked tools in the witch's arsenal, but they hold great power and knowledge. In some cultures, it is believed a spirit lives in the trees, known as a dryad. To avoid upsetting the dryad, knock on the wood of a tree before taking leaves, fruit, branches etc. This is where the superstition of "knock on wood" comes from.

Supplies
- A jar or container.
- Location of one of the following trees: alder, ash, beech, cypress, elder, fir, hawthorn, hazel, holly, magnolia, oak, palm, rowan, spruce, sycamore, walnut, or willow.
- Leaves from your chosen tree.
- Cinnamon.
- Clove.
- Coriander or cumin.
- Malachite gemstone.
- A black or white candle.

Instructions:
1. Find the location of one of the trees from the list above.
2. Walk around the tree three times.

3. Knock on the tree three times.
4. Pick leaves from the tree; between one and three should be enough.
5. Add your ingredients to the jar.
6. Close the lid and seal with wax.

Four Elements Protection Spell

This jar spell calls upon the power of the four elements to create a protection for yourself or others.

Supplies
- A jar or container.
- White salt.
- Four cloves.
- Five peppermint leaves.
- One teaspoon of dried rosemary.
- Two chamomile flowers.
- Moss agate gemstone.
- Blue lace agate gemstone.
- Smoky quartz gemstone.
- Lapis lazuli gemstone.
- White candle.

Instructions:
1. Pour a circle of white salt in a circle around your jar.
2. At the 12 o'clock position place four cloves and a moss agate gemstone.
3. At the 3 o'clock position place five peppermint leaves and a blue lace agate gemstone.
4. At the 6 o'clock position place one teaspoon of dried rosemary and a smoky quartz gemstone.
5. At the 9 o'clock position place two chamomile flowers and a lapis lazuli gemstone.
6. Starting with the midday position and working clockwise, add your ingredients to the jar.
7. Starting at the midday position and working clockwise, place the salt from the circle into the jar.
8. Close and seal with wax.

Invisibility Spell

A protection jar spell to make you "invisible" to someone so they bother you no more.

Supplies
- A jar or container.
- Lemon juice.
- Onion skins.
- Burnt matches.
- Black feathers.
- Water.
- Paper.
- Pen.
- String.

Instructions:
1. Write the name of the person on a slip of paper. If it is unsafe to use their name, use their initials or a code.
2. Wrap the paper around the three black feathers and tie with string.
3. Add the paper and feathers to the jar along with the other ingredients.
4. Add water to the jar.
5. Close the lid.
6. Shake the jar and repeat the following phrase nine times; "See me no more."
7. Store the jar away from your house.

Good Fortune and Luck Jar Spells

A Simple Good Luck Spell

This spell for good luck is easy to perform, but don't be fooled by its simplicity; it can still be highly effective. In fact, sometimes the most straightforward spells are the most powerful.

Supplies
- Jar or container.
- Paper.
- Pen.
- White salt.
- Uncooked rice.
- Sugar.
- Cinnamon.
- A green or white candle.

Instructions:
1. Take a slip of paper and write the following statement: "The tides of change will turn my way."
2. Fold the paper in half, towards you, with the intention of attracting good luck.
3. Continue to fold the paper again and again, still focussing on the intention of attracting good luck.
4. Place the paper in the jar.
5. Add the white salt, uncooked rice and ground cinnamon.
6. Close the jar and seal with wax.

Pulling Fortune and Favour Spell

A "pulling spell" pulls whatever it is you want, towards you. In this instance it's fortune and favour that's being pulled your way.

Supplies
- Jar or container.
- Paper.

- Pen.
- Sugar.
- Cloves.

Instructions:
1. Write your intention on a slip of paper. Make sure to use the present tense.
2. Fold the paper towards yourself and add it to the jar.
3. Add sugar and cloves.
4. Close the jar but do not seal it with wax. You want the spell to "expand" and not be trapped inside.
5. Every day, shake the jar and say your intention aloud or in your mind.

Peace and Prosperity Spell

A spell to encourage peace and prosperity in your life. In completing this spell, you can look forward to a period of success.

Supplies
- Jar or container.
- Uncooked green rice or white rice that has been dyed in green food colouring.
- Cinnamon.
- Bay leaf.
- Star anise.
- Aventurine gemstone.
- Pyrite gemstone.
- Citrine gemstone.
- A white or green candle.

Instructions:
1. Add the green rice to the bottom of the jar.
2. Add the cinnamon and star anise.
3. Burn the bay leaf, ensuring you catch the ash in the jar.
4. Add the gemstones.
5. Close the jar and seal with wax.

Monthly Full Moon Fortune Spell

As the name implies, this jar spell is to be performed on a full moon and will promote fortune and peace throughout the coming month.

Supplies
- Jar or container.
- Lemongrass.
- White salt.
- Sandalwood.
- Frankincense.
- Rosemary.
- Amethyst gemstone.
- Howlite gemstone.
- Blue candle.

Instructions:
1. Add your ingredients to the jar.
2. Close the jar and seal the jar with wax.
3. Repeat as needed on the full moon.

Abundance Spell

To have an abundance of something means to have plenty of it. In this case, abundance is being used to describe good fortune and having all that you need in life.

Supplies
- Jar or container.
- White salt.
- Mint leaves.
- Marigold flower.
- Ginger.
- Carnelian gemstone.
- Paper.
- Pen.
- Green candle.

Instructions:
1. Add the ingredients to the jar.
2. On a slip of paper write the mantra; "I have everything I need."
3. Add the paper to the jar and close the lid.
4. Seal the jar with wax.

Success Spell

Success means different things to different people; maybe success means getting that promotion at work, or finally asking your crush on a date, getting a high score on a test, or having the courage to speak up when you'd normally stay quiet. This success spell will help you achieve your goals, no matter what they may be. For added potency, perform during a waxing moon phase.

Supplies
- Jar or container.
- White salt.
- Bay leaf.
- Saffron.
- Poppy seeds.
- Malachite gemstone.
- Pen.

- Orange candle.

Instructions:
1. Write on the bay leaf a word that symbolises the area of your life in which you wish to see success; e.g. work, home, relationship, promotion, driving test, etc.
2. Burn the bay leaf, ensuring to catch the ash in the jar.
3. Add any unburnt bay lead to the jar.
4. Add the remaining ingredients.
5. Close the jar and seal with wax.

Eight Knots Spell

This spell is designed to bring you good luck.

Supplies
- Jar or container.
- White salt.
- Uncooked rice.
- Three bay leaves.
- A piece of string, twine or shoelace (no longer than 10 inches).
- Green candle.

Instructions:
1. Add the salt, rice and three bay leaves to the jar.
2. Take the string and tie eight knots in it.
3. Place the string in the jar.
4. Close the jar and seal with candle wax.

Green Salt Spell

The colour green has long been associated with luck and good fortune which is why this spell uses green salt.

Supplies
- Jar or container.
- Green salt.
- Bay leaf.

- Chamomile.
- Moss agate gemstone.
- Green candle.

Instructions:
1. Add the ingredients to the jar.
2. Close the lid and seal with candle wax.

Good Luck Spell

This jar spell brings good luck to all areas of your life.

Supplies
- Jar or container.
- Bladderwrack or seaweed.
- Chamomile.
- Comfrey.
- Jasmine.
- Bloodstone gemstone.
- Carnelian gemstone.
- Moss agate gemstone.
- A green or white candle.

Instructions:
1. Add the ingredients to the jar.
2. Close the jar and seal with candle wax.

Energetic Wake Up Spell

The energy around us can get stagnant; this jar spell is designed to "wake up" the tired energy and encourage the luck to start flowing our way again.

Supplies
- Jar or container.
- Cinnamon.
- Coffee beans or ground coffee.
- Basil.
- Nutmeg.

- Peppermint.
- Citrine gemstone.
- A gold, green or orange candle.

Instructions:
1. Add the ingredients to the jar.
2. Close the jar and seal with wax.
3. Give the jar a gentle shake when you feel the energy has dipped or stagnated.

Money and Wealth Jar Spells

Money Attraction Spell

This jar spell is best made on the New Moon or the first day of the month, and should be repeated regularly for maximum benefit.

Supplies
- Jar or container big enough for coins to fit inside.
- Ginger.
- Basil.
- Chamomile.
- Coins (loose change, small denominations are fine).
- Citrine or aventurine gemstone.
- Paper.
- Pen.
- A green or white candle.

Instructions:
1. Ensure the opening of your jar is big enough to fit coins through it.
2. Add the ginger, basil, chamomile and coins.
3. Add a citrine or aventurine gemstone, or both.
4. Take a slip of paper and write why you want to attract money into your life.
5. Fold the paper towards yourself.
6. Put the paper in the jar.
7. Seal the jar with candle wax.

Thirteen Pennies Spell

A traditional folk magic jar spell to encourage wealth.

Supplies
- Jar or container big enough for coins to fit inside.
- Water.
- 13 coins of any denomination.

- Cinnamon.
- Thyme.
- Basil.
- Cloves.
- Green candle.

Instructions:
1. Add water to the jar, followed by the coins and herbs.
2. Close the jar and seal with wax.
3. Meditate over the jar while you burn the rest of the candle; visualise wealth and prosperity.
4. Bury your jar in the ground or in a plant pot during the next full moon.

Money Altar Spell

This jar spell is designed to be a more permanent fixture in your home; either on your altar or in a space of its own.

Supplies
- Jar or container.
- Tray/plate.
- A place to keep the jar.
- Money, a larger denomination in a bill/note.
- White salt.
- Nutmeg.
- Peppermint.
- Ginger.
- Chamomile.
- Cinnamon.
- Bay leaf.
- Four pyrite gemstones.
- Aventurine gemstone.
- A green or white candle.

Instructions:
1. Perform the spell in the area you plan to keep the jar.
2. Place the bill/note in the centre of the plate.
3. Place the jar on top of the bill/note.
4. Around the edge of the plate place a ring of white salt.

5. On the 12 o'clock, 3 o'clock, 6 o'clock and 9 o'clock points of the salt circle, place a piece of pyrite.
6. Fill the jar with nutmeg, peppermint, ginger, chamomile, cinnamon and a bay leaf.
7. Add the aventurine gemstone to the jar.
8. Close the jar and seal with wax.
9. Use the hot wax to stick the candle to the top of the jar.
10. Burn the candle regularly to attract wealth.
11. Change the candle when needed.

Shake to Activate Spell

This jar spell can be shaken periodically to "wake up" the energy and further attract wealth into your life.

Supplies
- Jar or container.
- Cinnamon.
- Bay leaf.
- Basil.
- Chamomile.
- Pyrite gemstone.
- Green aventurine gemstone.
- Tiger's eye gemstone.
- Coins, any denomination.

Instructions:
1. Add the ingredients to the jar.
2. Close the lid but do not seal; you want the spell to "expand".

Five Times Five Spell

A traditional money spell based on numerology.

Supplies
- Jar or container.

- Money; specifically five different denominations, five of each denomination. E.g. 5 x 1p coins, 5 x 2p coins, 5 x 5p coins, 5 x 10p coins, 5 x 20p coins.
- Five kernels of dried corn.
- Five cloves.
- Five pecan nuts.

Instructions:
1. Place the ingredients into the jar.
2. Close the lid.
3. Gently shake the jar and say the following aloud; "Herbs, silver, copper and grain, work to increase my money gain."
4. Place the jar in your home and leave your wallet near it.

Money Tree Spell

Wealth is associated with the element of earth. This spell uses that connection to the earth element to "grow" your wealth.

Supplies
- Jar or container.
- Soil, earth or gravel from as near to your home as possible.
- A coin.
- A leaf of one of the following trees: ash, holly, rowan, or witch hazel.
- Hematite gemstone or smoky quartz gemstone.
- A black, green or white candle.

Instructions:
1. Place soil in the jar.
2. Push a coin down into the soil as though you are planting a seed.
3. Place the leaf and gemstone on top of the soil.
4. Close the jar and seal with wax.

Financial Security Spell

A lot of money jar spells focus on increasing and attracting wealth, but sometimes you might want financial security rather than increasing your money.

Supplies
- Jar or container.
- Pink salt.
- Cinnamon.
- Rosemary.
- Pink peppercorns.
- Green aventurine gemstone.

Instructions:
1. Place the ingredients in the jar.
2. Close the jar but do not seal with wax.

I.O.U. Spell

An I.O.U. is a phonetic acronym of the words "I owe you." It is considered a document that acknowledges the existence of a debt. In this spell you are creating an I.O.U. from the universe.

Supplies
- Jar or container.
- Paper.
- Pen.
- Basil.
- Chamomile.
- Marigold flower or poppy flower.
- A gold, green, purple or white candle.

Instructions:
1. On a slip of paper write the following; "IOU [the amount of money you require], signed The Universe".
2. Roll the paper.
3. Seal the paper with wax.
4. Put the paper in the jar with the ingredients.
5. Close the jar.
6. Seal with wax.

Jupiter Money Spell

Jupiter is associated with money, and so this jar spell uses items that correspond with the planet to heighten its power. For added potency, cast the spell on a Thursday.

Supplies
- Jar or container.
- White salt.
- Matches.
- A walnut.
- Lemon balm.
- Sage.
- A green, blue or purple candle.

Instructions:
1. Take a deep breath and breathe out into the jar four times.
2. Add white salt.
3. Light a match and drop it into the jar, on top of the white salt.
4. Lay the lid of the jar over the jar, but do not seal. You want to keep as much of the smoke in the jar as possible, but still be able to add the rest of your ingredients.
5. Lift the lid and quickly add the walnut, lemon balm and sage, and close the lid.
6. Seal the jar with wax.

Money Powder Spell

Unlike many of the other jar spells in this book, which remain sealed, this jar spell is designed to be opened and used often.

Supplies
- Jar or container.
- Mortar and pestle, or grinder.
- Chamomile.
- Cinnamon.
- Cloves.
- Parsley.
- Aventurine gemstone.

Instructions:

1. Grind the dried chamomile, cinnamon, cloves and parsley into a powder.
2. Add the powder to a jar.
3. Place the aventurine gemstone inside the powder.
4. On the first of the month, open the jar and sprinkle the powder outside your front door.

Confidence Jar Spells

A Simple Confidence Spell

If you are looking for self-confidence, this jar spell is best made on Sundays. If you are looking for confidence in romantic relationships, make the jar spell on Fridays. If you are looking for confidence at work, make the jar spell on Wednesdays.

Supplies
- Jar or container.
- Chamomile.
- Dried orange peel.
- Black salt.
- Amethyst gemstone.
- A gold candle or gold ribbon.

Instructions:
1. As you add each ingredient, hold it in your hands first and focus on drawing confidence towards you and the ingredient.
2. Add the black salt first, then the amethyst, orange peel and chamomile.
3. Seal the jar with gold wax, or tie a golden ribbon around it.

Sun Water Confidence Spell

This jar spell is best made on Sundays as this day is associated with the sun. To make Sun Water; leave a jar/cup of water in direct sunlight, and bring indoors before nightfall. Sun water collected in the months of June, July or August is the most powerful.

Supplies
- Jar or container.
- Sugar.
- Cinnamon.
- Sun water.

Instructions:

1. Add sugar followed by cinnamon.
2. Pour in the sun water.
3. Close the jar.
4. From sunrise to sunset, leave this jar in direct sunlight.
5. Shake whenever you need more confidence.

Boosting the Confidence of Others Spell

Creating a jar spell to boost the confidence of a family member or friend is a generous and kind act that will be rewarded spiritually.

Supplies
- Jar or container.
- Nettle.
- Sage.
- Carnation, honeysuckle or geranium flower.
- Sodalite gemstone.
- Rose quartz gemstone.
- Paper.
- Pen.
- Pink candle.

Instructions:
1. Add the ingredients to the jar along with the gemstones.
2. On a slip of paper write the name or initials of the person in question.
3. Add the paper to the jar and close the lid.
4. Seal the jar with a pink candle.

Building Courage Spell

Building courage can be difficult; whether you're starting a new job, facing health problems or working through personal issues. This spell is designed to help you build courage through the use of your favourite flower or a flower that grows near to your home. This will ground you, physically and metaphysically, as you work through your challenges.

Supplies
- Jar or container.

- Your favourite flower, or a flower that grows near to where you live; dried.
- Rosemary.
- Carnelian gemstone.
- Obsidian gemstone.

Instructions:
1. Ensure the flowers are fully dry before starting the spell.
2. Add your ingredients to the jar; do not be afraid to fill this jar to the brim.
3. Close the lid and place somewhere in your home where you can admire it.

Go Your Own Way Spell

This spell encourages you to have the confidence and inner-strength to "go your own way"; whether that be leaving a bad relationship, making a decision for yourself, or taking a chance on a dream you have.

Supplies
- Jar or container.
- Fireproof bowl.
- Matches or a lighter.
- Paper.
- Pen.
- A white or purple candle.
- Basil.
- Rose petals.
- Rosemary.

Instructions:
1. On a slip of paper write the following statement; "I demand you step away from my life. Free me from this constant strife. I reclaim my mind and soul, rejecting your influence and becoming whole".
2. Light a white or purple candle.
3. Place the paper in the bowl and burn the paper with the flame of the candle. Focus on your intention.
4. Collect any ash or unburnt paper in the jar.
5. Add the remaining ingredients.
6. Close the jar and seal with wax.

First Impressions Spell

This jar spell can be used before meeting someone new; this could be before an interview, a date, or attending a social event. It works to boost your confidence and create an air of credence around you.

Supplies
- Jar or container.
- Dried orange peel.
- Rose petals.
- Nettle leaves.
- Vanilla pods.
- White candle.

Instructions:
1. Add your ingredients to the jar.
2. Close the lid and seal with wax.

Work and Career Jar Spells

Manifesting Your Dream Job Spell

This spell is best performed on a new moon or a waxing moon phase.

Supplies
- Jar or container.
- Bluebells.
- Chamomile.
- Lavender.
- Patchouli.
- Citrine gemstone.
- Paper.
- Pen.
- A white or purple candle.

Instructions:
1. Add the ingredients to the jar.
2. On a slip of paper write your dream job 12 times.
3. Fold the paper towards yourself, envisioning yourself in the job.
4. Add the paper to the jar.
5. Close the lid and seal with wax.

Career Success Spell

A jar spell to encourage success at work. It is best performed on a Wednesday as that is the day associated with careers and work.

Supplies
- Jar or container.
- Spiral shaped pasta, uncooked.
- Rosemary.
- Peony or bluebell.
- Blackberry.
- A brown, gold or green candle.

Instructions:
1. Place the ingredients in the jar with the uncooked pasta at the bottom.
2. Close the jar and seal with wax.
3. For added potency, bury under any of the following trees: apple, cedar, elder, hawthorn, oak, or palm.

A Raise at Work Spell

A jar spell to help you achieve a raise at work by using ingredients that correspond to wealth, abundance, manifestation, and confidence.

Supplies
- Jar or container.
- Cinnamon.
- Ginger.
- Bluebell or honeysuckle.
- Maple or sycamore leaves.
- Chamomile.
- Lavender.
- Rosemary.
- Thyme.
- White candle.

Instructions:
1. Place the ingredients in a jar.
2. Close the jar and seal with wax.
3. Keep the jar at work, or if that's not possible, keep it next to your front door so you can shake it before you leave for work.

Positivity in the Workplace Spell

Workplaces and work colleagues can sometimes be toxic; people trying to get ahead, jealousy, and gossip. This spell will help you rise above the bad energies and protect you from harm whilst at work.

Supplies
- Jar or container.

- Basil.
- Raspberry leaves.
- Spearmint or peppermint leaves.
- Catnip.
- Sage.
- Chamomile.
- Blue lace agate gemstone.
- White candle.

Instructions:
1. Place the ingredients in the jar.
2. Close the lid and seal with wax.

Increased Productivity Spell

This spell is best cast on a Wednesday as it's the middle of the working week and when people feel the least productive.

Supplies
- Jar or container.
- Peppermint.
- Cinnamon.
- Thyme.
- Heather or lilac.
- Basil.
- Poppy petals or seeds.
- A blue, purple, yellow or white candle.

Instructions:
1. Place the ingredients in the jar.
2. Close the lid and seal with wax.
3. Keep the jar at work, or if that is not possible, by your front door so you can shake it before you go to work.

Self Improvement Jar Spells

Anti-Anxiety Spell

This jar spell is best made on Saturdays or Sundays. Saturdays are associated with personal goals and releasing bad habits, and Sundays are associated with the healing of the body, mind and soul. For added potency, choose a time when the moon is waning as this symbolises pushing the anxiety away from you.

Supplies
- Jar or container.
- Eucalyptus.
- White salt.
- Lavender.
- Chamomile.
- Moonstone and/or blue lace agate gemstone.
- Paper.
- Pen.

Instructions:
1. Add the ingredients into the jar with the care and love you wish to have for yourself.
2. Write a personal mantra on a slip of paper and add it to the jar.

Sleep Well Spell

Let go of your worries and have a restful night sleep with this jar spell. In this spell you will be securing a candle to the inside bottom of the jar. The candle will need to be short enough to fit inside the jar with the lid on. You will also need to ensure any flammable ingredients are not at risk of catching on fire.

Supplies
- Jar or container.
- Lavender.
- Pink salt.
- Basil.
- Thyme.

- A white, black or brown candle.
- Adhesive putty such as "Blu Tac".

Instructions:
1. Using the adhesive putty, secure your candle to the inside bottom of the jar.
2. Around the base of the candle, inside the jar, place your ingredients.
3. Light the candle.
4. Meditate for a moment on letting go of your worries and imagine yourself drifting off to sleep.
5. When you are ready, close the lid of the jar and watch the flame extinguish itself, before heading to bed.

Inner Peace Spell

Find your inner peace with this jar spell. Best made on Sundays or during a waxing moon phase.

Supplies
- Jar or container.
- Beach sand, river silt, or soil from your garden/local park.
- Bergamot.
- Dried coconut.
- White salt.
- Blue lace agate gemstone.

Instructions:
1. Add the ingredients to the jar and close the lid.
2. Shake the jar to reactivate.

Focus for Studying Spell

This jar spell is perfect for those studying at school and college, or when you need help retaining important information.

Supplies
- Jar or container.
- Bay leaf.
- Coffee.
- Ginger.

- Lilac.
- Allspice or a mixture of gloves, nutmeg and cinnamon.

Instructions:
1. Burn the bay leaf, and as you do, see yourself studying and absorbing the information with ease.
2. Collect the ash in the jar along with any bay leaf that was unburnt.
3. Add the other ingredients.

Enhance Creativity Spell

Enhance your creativity and nurture your creative spirit with this jar spell.

Supplies
- Jar or container.
- White salt.
- Lemongrass.
- Dried apple.
- Cherry blossoms.
- Star anise.
- Calcite gemstone.
- Paper.
- Pen.
- White candle.

Instructions:
1. Add the ingredients to the jar.
2. On a slip of paper write the following mantra; "I am an empty vessel into which creativity flows."
3. Add the paper to the jar and close the lid.
4. Seal the jar with candle wax.

Finding Balance Spell

Our lives can be hectic, and it can sometimes feel as though we are spiralling out of control. This jar spell will help you find balance in your life; whether that be a work/life balance or finding more time for your hobbies.

Supplies
- Jar or container.
- White salt.
- Chives.
- Aniseed.
- Geranium.
- Amazonite gemstone.
- Paper.
- Pen.

Instructions:
1. Add the ingredients to the jar.
2. On a slip of paper write the following manta; "I have balance in my life."
3. Add the paper to the jar and close the lid.

Adventure and Excitement Spell

When you feel that life is stale and you're stuck in your ways, it can be hard to feel motivated. This spell encourages adventure into your life. Be sure to cleanse your space, tools and ingredients before starting the spell so as to attract only fun and positive adventures.

Supplies
- Jar or container.
- White salt.
- Ginseng.
- Cardamon.
- Moonstone gemstone.
- Paper.
- Pen.
- Red candle.

Instructions:
1. Add the ingredients to the jar.
2. On a slip of paper write the following mantra; "I am open to new possibilities."
3. Add the paper to the jar and close the lid.
4. Seal the jar with candle wax.

Harmony Spell

In musical terms; a harmony is when singers or musicians produce multiple sounds and notes that fit together to create something bigger and more beautiful. This jar spell creates the same effect in your life; bringing together all the pieces of you and your life to create something greater than the sum of its parts.

Supplies
- Jar or container.
- White salt.
- Daisy, honeysuckle or rose.
- Violets.
- Cardamon.
- Aquamarine gemstone.
- Paper.
- Pen.
- A blue or green candle.

Instructions:
1. Add the ingredients to the jar.
2. On a slip of paper write the following mantra; "My life is a beautiful melody carried on the winds."
3. Add the paper to the jar and close the lid.
4. Seal the jar with candle wax.

Productivity Spell

We can't be our best productive selves all the time; give this jar a little shake when you need a boost of productivity.

Supplies
- Jar or container.
- White salt.
- Rosemary.
- Vanilla.
- Cloves.
- Obsidian gemstone.
- Paper.

- Pen.
- A gold or yellow candle.

Instructions:
1. Add the ingredients to the jar.
2. On a slip of paper write the following mantra; "I am organised and focussed."
3. Add the paper to the jar and close the lid.
4. Seal the jar with candle wax.

Physical Health Spell

This jar spell promotes physical health. For the best results, perform on Sundays.

Supplies
- Jar or container.
- White salt.
- Eucalyptus.
- Sage.
- Cinnamon.
- Amethyst gemstone.
- Paper.
- Pen.
- An orange, red or white candle.

Instructions:
1. Add the ingredients to the jar.
2. On a slip of paper write the following mantra; "I look after my body. My body is strong and healthy."
3. Add the paper to the jar and close the lid.
4. Seal the jar with candle wax.

Coping with Grief Spell

This jar spell helps ease the pain of grief and loss.

Supplies
- Jar or container.
- Black salt.
- Myrrh.
- Aloe vera.
- Rose petals.
- Rose quartz gemstone.
- White candle.

Instructions:
1. Add the ingredients to the jar.
2. Close the jar and seal with wax.
3. Rub the jar when you need relief from the pain of grief.

Love and Relationships Jar Spells

———————❖———————

Improving Relationships Spell

This jar spell can be used to improve your relationship with friends or family, and works by encouraging you to be the best friend, sister, brother or partner that you can be.

Supplies
- Jar or container.
- White salt.
- Coriander.
- Lemon peel.
- Patchouli.
- Ginger.
- Tigers Eye gemstone.
- Paper.
- Pen.
- A blue or red candle.

Instructions:
1. Add the ingredients.
2. On a slip of paper write the following manta, "I strive to be the best [partner/friend/sister] I can be."
3. Add the slip of paper to the jar.
4. Seal the jar with a candle.

A Powerful and Intense Love Spell

This jar spell is best made on Fridays as this is the day associated with love. For extra potency, choose a Friday that coincides with a waxing moon phase.

Supplies
- Jar or container.
- Pink himalayan salt.
- Patchouli incense.

- Vanilla extract.
- Nutmeg.
- Dried rose petals.
- Whole, dried bay leaf.
- Pen.
- Honey or agave.
- Sugar.
- Rose quartz.
- A red or pink candle.

Instructions:
1. Ensure the table/surface is clear of any debris.
2. Light the candle.
3. Place your jar on the table and sprinkle a circle of pink himalayan salt around it.
4. Light the patchouli incense and cleanse the jar.
5. Add vanilla extract to the jar followed by nutmeg and dried rose petals.
6. On the bay leaf, write the name of the persons whom you wish to fall in love.
7. Burn the bay leaf, ensuring any ash or unburnt bay leaf goes into the jar.
8. Add honey/agave, followed by sugar.
9. Add rose quartz to the jar.
10. Close the jar and seal with the wax from the candle.
11. Bury the jar under any of the following trees: apple, cherry, chestnut, elder, elm, maple, pomegranate, or willow.

Love Amplification Spell

This jar spell is designed to amplify love and care in an already blossoming relationship; whether that be romantic, platonic, or familial.

Supplies
- Jar or container.
- White salt.
- Lavender.
- Rose petals.
- Dried apple or apple seeds.
- Rose quartz.

- Pen.
- Paper.
- Pink candle.

Instructions:
1. Add the ingredients to the jar.
2. On a slip of paper write the following mantra; "I open my heart to love. Others open their hearts to my love. Our love flows through one another freely."
3. Fold the paper towards yourself as many times as needed.
4. Add the paper to the jar and close the lid.
5. Seal the jar with candle wax.

Self Love Spell

Loving ourselves can be difficult. Oftentimes we let the little voice in our head say all kinds of hideous things about us, but remember; that voice lies. You are worthy of love and care. This spell will help to quieten that little voice and promote self love.

Supplies
- Jar or container.
- Sugar.
- Lavender.
- Hibiscus.
- Rosehip.
- Rose quartz gemstone.
- Moonstone gemstone.
- A white or pink candle.

Instructions:
1. Add the ingredients to the jar and close the lid.
2. Light the candle and focus on the flame.
3. Imagine the light and heat of the candle is fuelling your spiritual body, filling you with light and love.
4. Seal the jar with the candle wax.
5. Shake or rub the jar whenever you need reminding of your worth.

First Date Confidence Spell

This jar spell is perfect for boosting your confidence before a first date (or any date) with someone. For added potency, perform on a Friday.

Supplies
- Jar or container.
- White salt.
- Cherry blossoms.
- Apple tree leaves.
- Nettle leaves.
- Basil.
- Carnelian gemstone or tiger's eye gemstone.
- Pink or red ribbon/string.
- White candle.

Instructions:
1. Add the white salt, cherry blossoms, apple tree leaves, nettle, basil and gemstones to the jar.
2. Close the lid.
3. Tie the ribbon or string around the place where the lid meets the jar.
4. Seal the jar with wax.

Quality Over Quantity Spell

This jar spell attracts quality relationships into your life; it is often considered better to have a few good friends rather than many acquaintances. This spell can also be applied to lovers if you are actively dating.

Supplies
- Jar or container.
- Pink himalayan salt.
- 13 coriander seeds.
- Blackberry leaves.
- Rose petals.
- Basil.
- Dandelion flower.
- Rose quartz gemstone.
- Pink or red ribbon/string.

- Paper.
- Pen.
- A red or pink candle.

Instructions:
1. Write on a slip of paper the following statement; "I accept nothing less than healthy, balanced love."
2. Fold the paper towards yourself.
3. Add the paper and ingredients to the jar.
4. Close the jar.
5. Tie ribbon or string around the container, where the lid meets the jar.
6. Seal the jar with wax.

Attracting New Lovers Spell

This jar spell is ideal for attracting potential lovers into your life. For added potency, cast the spell on a waxing moon phase and/or a Friday.

Supplies
- Jar or container.
- Pink himalayan salt.
- Rose petals.
- Hibiscus flowers.
- Lavender.
- Cinnamon.
- Cardamom.
- Honey.
- Red candle.

Instructions:
1. Add the salt, rose petals, hibiscus, lavender, cinnamon and cardamom to the jar.
2. Add the honey last.
3. Close the jar and seal with wax.

Healing After a Break Up Spell

This jar spell will help you move on after heartbreak. The ideal time to cast this spell is during a waning moon phase or a new moon.

Supplies
- Jar or container.
- Comfrey.
- Rosemary.
- Dandelion flower.
- Vervain.
- A black, grey or white candle.

Instructions:
1. Add the ingredients to the jar.
2. Close the lid and seal with wax.
3. Bury the jar under any of the following trees: apple, ash, elder, elm, juniper, hazel holly or oak.

Restore Love Spell

This spell is designed to heal the wounds of a broken friendship or relationship. Perhaps you had an argument, or perhaps you grew apart over time; in either case, this jar spell will aid in its repair.

Supplies
- Jar or container.
- Two pieces of string/twine, in two different colours.
- Basil.
- Sage.
- Daisy flowers.
- Chamomile.
- Lavender.
- Lemon balm.
- A white, purple or pink candle.

Instructions:
1. Add the basil, sage, daisies, chamomile, lavender and lemon balm to the jar.

2. Take the two pieces of string and hold them in your hand, side by side.
3. Tie nine knots along the strings; tying them together.
4. With each knot you make, say the following, "Knot of love/friendship, mend and rewrite."
5. Add the knotted strings to the jar.
6. Close the jar and seal with wax.

Burning Heartbreak Spell

Using the element of fire, this spell will vanquish heartbreak. Using the element of earth, this spell will heal and mend.

Supplies
- Jar or container.
- Fire safe bowl.
- Matches.
- A photo of you.
- A photo of the person who has broken your heart.
- White salt.
- Feverfew.
- Gardenia.
- Lavender.
- Lemon balm.
- Aventurine gemstone.
- Lapis lazuli gemstone.
- A blue or white candle.

Instructions:
1. Add the salt, flowers and herbs to the jar.
2. Light a match and set fire to the photographs. Put them in the bowl to burn.
3. Collect the ash into the jar.
4. Cover with the other ingredients.
5. Close the jar and seal with wax.
6. Bury under any of the following trees: apple, ash, birch, Cedar, elder, hazel, holly, oak, or walnut.

House and Home Jar Spells

Happy Home Spell

Are you experiencing an unbalanced or unharmonious home? Perhaps your family is arguing, or people cannot see eye to eye. This jar spell will help to calm the energy in your home. This jar spell is designed to stay in the home and look like a beautiful decoration, so place your items in the jar in a pleasing way. Ensure the ingredients and jar are dry, or else they will decompose.

Supplies
- Jar or container.
- Pink salt.
- Eucalyptus.
- Lavender.
- Dried orange peel.
- Carnelian gemstone.
- Rose quartz gemstone.
- Paper.
- Pen.

Instructions:
1. Place the jar on the table.
2. Lay your ingredients around the jar in a semi-circle.
3. One by one, add the ingredients into the jar.
4. Finally, write your intention on a slip of paper.
5. Roll the paper and place it in the jar.
5. Close your jar and place it in your home.

Home Protection Spell

The jar spell requires multiple jars that will be hung around the home, so I suggest very small jars. Your ingredients will also need to be 100% dry to avoid mould. If your ingredients do start to mould, despite the ingredients being dry, this means the jar has caught bad energy and the jar should be re-made. For the best results, use these jar spells on the doors that see the most traffic in the home.

Supplies
- Multiple jars, small size.
- Twine, string or ribbon.
- Sage.
- Saint John's Wort.
- Rose petals.
- Broken egg shells.
- White salt.

Instructions:
1. Place your ingredients inside the jars, making sure to do each jar's ingredients in the same order.
2. Once sealed, hang the jars from the door frames using a twine or ribbon.

Incense Home Protection Spell

In this jar spell, the cleansing is part of the ritual so make sure to follow the instructions.

Supplies
- Jar or container.
- An incense stick in your chosen smell.
- Black pepper.
- White salt.
- Rosemary.
- Cloves.
- Smoky quartz gemstone.
- Amethyst gemstone.

Instructions
1. Light the incense stick.
2. Place the lit incense into the jar and rotate it 11 times in a clockwise direction.
3. Place the incense stick in a holder to continue burning.
4. As you add each ingredient, say the following, "Guard my home and all within".

5. Finally, place the incense back into the jar and "catch" the smoke with the lid; sealing it inside.

Peaceful Home Spell

A simple jar spell that is best done on Saturdays or during a new moon.

Supplies
- Jar or container.
- Dust and dirt from around your home.
- Tap water from your home.
- Lemon peel.
- Rose petals or rose oil.
- White candle.

Instructions
1. Place all your ingredients in the jar and close the lid.
2. Light the candle and drop wax on the lid; whilst the wax is still hot, attach the candle to the lid.
3. Let the candle burn down upon the top of the jar.

Unwanted Visitors Spell

A jar spell for if someone has outstayed their welcome.

Supplies
- Jar or container.
- Agrimony.
- Basil.
- Clover.
- Rosemary.
- Peppermint.
- Nettle leaf.
- A black, green or purple candle.

Instructions
1. Add the ingredients to the jar.
2. Close and seal with wax.

Metaphysics and Magic Jar Spells

━━━━ ✛ ━━━━

Enhance Your Metaphysical Magnetism Spell

This spell jar and its ingredients are designed to draw magical energy towards you, with the intention of making it easier to cast spells going forward.

Supplies
- Jar or container.
- A clipping of your hair.
- Rose petals.
- Cinnamon.
- Mint leaves.
- Clear quartz gemstone.
- Rose quartz gemstone.
- Tigers eye gemstone.
- Pyrite gemstone.
- Sunstone gemstone.

Instructions:
1. On the night before the full moon, sleep with the four gemstones under your pillow.
2. On the night of the full moon, collect your ingredients and tools ready to perform the spell.
3. Thoroughly cleanse the space, tools and ingredients.
4. Add the rose petals first and lay your hair upon them.
5. Add the remaining ingredients and gemstones.
6. Close the jar.
7. Leave this jar in direct moonlight every full moon to recharge, and bring it back inside before dawn.

Spiritually Healing Spell

Creating and casting spells can take its toll on even the most talented witch. This restorative jar spell helps to heal your spiritual self when you feel depleted of energy. This spell is best performed on full moons, Sundays or the first day of the new month.

Supplies
- Jar or container.
- Lavender.
- Cloves of garlic.
- Pink himalayan salt.
- Chamomile.
- Amber or carnelian gemstone.
- Turmeric.

Instructions:
1. Add your ingredients to the jar.
2. For added potency, add a personal item of yours to the jar such as hair or an item of jewellery.

Welcoming the Spirits Spell

A jar spell that sends a friendly and welcoming energetic greeting to the spirit world; perfect for hedge witches and those wishing to work with ancestors.

Supplies
- Jar or container.
- Black pepper.
- Cinnamon.
- Sprig of fir tree.
- Angelica root or yarrow.
- Amethyst gemstone.
- Labradorite gemstone.
- Moonstone gemstone.
- Paper.
- Pen.
- Purple candle.

Instructions:
1. Add the black pepper, cinnamon, fir tree and angelica root/yarrow to the jar.
2. Add the gemstones.
3. Light a candle and drip the melting wax into the jar.
4. Write a letter to the spirits you wish to contact, welcoming them and asking permission to make contact.

5. Fold/roll the letter and seal with wax.
6. Place the letter in the jar.
7. Put the lid on the jar and seal with wax.
8. Attach the candle to the lid of the jar and let it burn down.

Wisdom Spell

This jar spell will encourage the experience, knowledge and good judgement associated with wisdom.

Supplies
- Jar or container.
- White salt.
- Parsley.
- Lilac.
- Cumin.
- Lapis lazuli gemstone.
- Paper.
- Pen.
- Blue candle.

Instructions:
1. Add the ingredients to the jar.
2. On a slip of paper write the following mantra; "I am learning, I am growing."
3. Add the paper to the jar and close the lid.
4. Seal the jar with candle wax.

Uncovering Your Destiny Spell

If you are feeling spiritually lost and need direction; try this jar spell. For best results, perform on a new moon.

Supplies
- Jar or container.
- Honeysuckle flower.
- Flax seeds.
- Moonstone gemstone.

- Labradorite gemstone.
- Purple candle.

Instructions:
1. Add the ingredients to the jar.
2. Leave the jar in moon light every night, bringing it in before dawn.
3. On the full moon, bury the jar under a blackthorn tree or honeysuckle plant.

Beseech the Psychopomp Spell

A psychopomp is a conductor of souls; a spirit who guides the soul between the land of the living and the land of the dead. If you have recently lost a loved one, this jar spell will call out to the psychopomp leading their soul, and ask them to do so with kindness and compassion.

Supplies
- Jar or container.
- Chamomile.
- Jasmine.
- Lavender.
- Blackberry leaf.
- Yarrow.
- Paper.
- Pen.
- A black, purple, red or white candle.

Instructions:
1. Write the name of the recently deceased loved one on a slip of paper ten times.
2. Fold the paper and add to the jar.
3. Add the remaining ingredients.
4. Close the jar.
5. Using hot wax from the candle, drip some wax onto the lid of the jar and stick the candle to the top.
6. Let the candle burn down over ten nights.
7. Each night, when you light the candle, take a moment to focus on your loved one and their safe passage to the other side.

Scrying Spell

Scrying is a type of divination; a way to see into the future and gain insight. Scrying is often done with bowls or mirrors, but a jar can also be used.

Supplies
- Jar or container; must be clear glass, fairly large, with no logos/stickers/brand names on the base.
- Bowl or container suitable for holding boiling liquid.
- Moon water.
- Hibiscus.
- Peppermint leaves.
- Mugwort.
- Tea strainer or a cloth for straining liquid.

Instructions:
1. Boil the moon water either in a kettle or on the stove.
2. Place your hibiscus, peppermint leaves and mugwort into a container suitable for boiling water.
3. Pour the water over the herbs and let them steep until the water turns dark and cools.
4. Using a tea strainer or a cloth, strain the cooled liquid into your jar. You can dispose of the used plants.
5. Close the jar but do not seal with wax.
6. On the full moon, leave your scrying jar in direct moonlight to recharge.
7. When you are ready to scry; sit in a dimly lit room, and place the jar on a table.
8. Place three lit candles in a triangular shape around the jar.
9. Relax your gaze and focus into the water.
10. After some time and some practice you will start to see shapes and vision appearing in the water, giving hints to what is to come and answers to your questions.

Dreamwork Spell

Many magical practitioners engage in dreamwork; a type of lucid dreaming in which the sleeper is able to work magic from inside their slumber. Witches who practise dreamwork tend to believe that dreams are not merely inside our minds, but a higher plain of existence where our magical working is amplified. This jar spell is designed to aid you in finding this "dream land".

Supplies
- Jar or container.
- Angelica.
- Bergamot.
- Catnip.
- Heliotrope.
- Yarrow.
- A black, blue, purple or yellow candle.

Instructions:
1. Place your ingredients in a jar.
2. Close the lid and seal with wax.
3. Rub the side of the jar in a clockwise direction two times before bed.
4. Keep the jar under your bed while you sleep.

Recharge Your Power Spell

The sun is often overlooked by those new to magical practice. There is a great emphasis put on the moon and its power, but we should not forget that the sun is just as powerful. The sun is associated with the energy of consciousness, wellbeing, and confidence. It can help you strengthen already positive energies and recharge your metaphysical body.

Supplies
- Jar or container.
- A sprig from any of the following trees; ash, cedar, juniper, oak, pal, rowan or walnut.
- Sunflower seeds or a whole sunflower head.
- Daffodil.
- Daisies.
- Chamomile.
- Any of the following gemstones; carnelian, citrine, clear quartz, sunstone or tiger's eye.
- Sunflower oil or olive oil.
- Apple cider vinegar.
- A gold, orange or yellow candle.

Instructions:
1. Place the ingredients in the jar.
2. Pour oil over the ingredients ensuring they are completely covered.
3. Add some apple cider vinegar.
4. Close the jar and seal with wax.
5. Leave the jar in warm sunlight and bring it in at night.

Divination Jar Spell

Divination is the practice of telling the future by supernatural means. The commonly used form of divination is tarot cards, but there are many other ways. This jar spell shows you how to make a "divination jar". It will require you to collect a number of charms, items, trinkets or dried flowers that you assign a certain meaning to. You can choose which items are assigned to which meaning.

Supplies
- Jar or container; must be opaque or lined so you can not see inside.
- A charm, item, trinket or dried flower for each of the following: self, health, wealth, family, love, friends, strength, creativity, patience, self-care, trust, balance, goals.

Instructions:
1. Place your items in the jar.
2. Close the lid but do not seal.
3. When it is time to divine, gently shake the jar, open the lid, and pour the contents onto a clean surface.
4. Look at the items and assess the situation; where is the self in all this? What items are closer to or further away from others?
5. Make notes on what you see and reflect on your results. Divination takes practice and the results may not always be clear at first.
6. To recharge your jar, place it under the light of a full moon.

Wheel of the Year Jar Spells

———✦———

Imbolc Blessing Spell

Imbolc is a holiday celebrated from sunrise on February 1 through sunset on February 2. Based on a Celtic tradition, Imbolc marks the halfway point between Yule (Winter Solstice) and Ostara (Spring Equinox).

Imbolc is about purification, cleansing, and clearing away stagnation that has built up over the winter months.

Create this jar spell during sunrise of February 1 and it will bring good fortune and blessings over the spring period. If you have an altar in your home, place this jar on the altar.

Supplies
- Jar or container.
- Basil.
- Cinnamon.
- Blackberry leaves.
- Snowdrop flowers.
- Crocus petals.
- Amethyst gemstone.
- Moonstone gemstone.
- Blue candle.

Instructions:
1. Sit in a North-Easterly direction.
2. Place the open jar on the table or surface on which you are working.
3. Lay your ingredients in a circle around the jar with the candle in the 12 o'clock position to the jar.
4. Light the candle.
5. One by one, take your ingredients and place them in the jar.
6. Close the jar and seal it with wax.

Ostara Blessing Spell

Ostara is a holiday celebrated anywhere from March 19 to March 22 (the dates change slightly each year). It marks the Spring Equinox; the first day of spring.

Imbolc is about birth and rebirth, change, growing in strength, preparation and new beginnings.

Create this jar spell at dawn on Ostara and it will bring good fortune and blessings over the spring period. If you have an altar in your home, place this jar on the altar.

Supplies
- Jar or container.
- Crocus.
- Daffodil.
- Tulip.
- Aventurine gemstone.
- Bloodstone gemstone.
- Citrine gemstone.
- Green candle.

Instructions:
1. Sit in an Easterly direction.
2. Place the open jar on the table or surface on which you are working.
3. Lay your ingredients in a circle around the jar with the candle in the 12 o'clock position to the jar.
4. Light the candle.
5. One by one, take your ingredients and place them in the jar.
6. Close the jar and seal it with wax.

Beltane Blessing Spell

Beltane is a holiday celebrated on May 1. It falls midway between Ostara (Spring Equinox) and Litha (Summer Solstice). It is commonly regarded as the first day of summer.

Beltane is about abundance, creation, growth, love, lust, and growth.

Create this jar spell at dawn on Beltane and it will bring good fortune and blessings over the summer period. If you have an altar in your home, place this jar on the altar.

Supplies
- Jar or container.
- Daisy.
- Honeysuckle.
- Ivy.
- Violet.
- Lemon peel.
- Mint.
- Oak leaves.
- Purple candle.

Instructions:
1. Sit in a South-Easterly direction.
2. Place the open jar on the table or surface on which you are working.
3. Lay your ingredients in a circle around the jar with the candle in the 12 o'clock position to the jar.
4. Light the candle.
5. One by one, take your ingredients and place them in the jar.
6. Close the jar and seal it with wax.

Litha Blessing Spell

Litha is a holiday celebrated between June 19 and June 22 (the dates change slightly each year). It marks the Summer Solstice; one of two days in the year when day and night are the same length.

Litha is about abundance, growth, healing, power, and success.

Create this jar spell at dawn Litha and it will bring good fortune and blessings over the summer period. If you have an altar in your home, place this jar on the altar.

Supplies
- Jar or container.
- Foxglove.

- Carnation.
- Ginger.
- Peppermint.
- Carnelian gemstone.
- Obsidian gemstone.
- Tiger's eye gemstone.
- Red candle.

Instructions:
1. Sit in a South facing direction.
2. Place the open jar on the table or surface on which you are working.
3. Lay your ingredients in a circle around the jar with the candle in the 12 o'clock position to the jar.
4. Light the candle.
5. One by one, take your ingredients and place them in the jar.
6. Close the jar and seal it with wax.

Lughnasadh Blessing Spell

Lughnasadh is a holiday celebrated on August 1. It marks the halfway point between Litha (Summer Solstice) and Mabon (Autumn Equinox). It is considered the beginning of autumn and the harvest season.

Lughnasadh is about ancestors, heritage, introspection, reflection, and blessings.

Create this jar spell at dusk on Lughnasadh and it will bring good fortune and blessings over the autumn period. If you have an altar in your home, place this jar on the altar.

Supplies
- Jar or container.
- Basil.
- Bay leaf.
- Fennel.
- Rosemary.
- Citrine gemstone.
- Onyx gemstone.
- Smoky quartz.

- A gold or yellow candle.

Instructions:
1. Sit in a South-Westerly direction.
2. Place the open jar on the table or surface on which you are working.
3. Lay your ingredients in a circle around the jar with the candle in the 12 o'clock position to the jar.
4. Light the candle.
5. One by one, take your ingredients and place them in the jar.
6. Close the jar and seal it with wax.

Mabon Blessing Spell

Mabon is a holiday usually celebrated between September 21 and September 24 (the dates vary slightly each year). It marks the Autumn Equinox.

Mabon is about accomplishment, gratitude, healing, ancestors, and sharing.

Create this jar spell at dusk on Mabon and it will bring good fortune and blessings over the autumn period. If you have an altar in your home, place this jar on the altar.

Supplies
- Jar or container.
- Acorns.
- Ivy.
- Myrrh.
- Sage.
- Amber.
- Hematite.
- Blue candle.

Instructions:
1. Sit in a West facing direction.
2. Place the open jar on the table or surface on which you are working.
3. Lay your ingredients in a circle around the jar with the candle in the 12 o'clock position to the jar.
4. Light the candle.
5. One by one, take your ingredients and place them in the jar.

6. Close the jar and seal it with wax.

Samhain Blessing Spell

Samhain is a holiday celebrated on October 31 and is often described as "Witches New Year". It marks the time when the veil between the world of living and the world of the dead is thinnest.

Samhain is about ancestry, courage, change, other worlds, survival, and magic.

Create this jar spell at midnight on the full moon before Samhain and it will bring good fortune and blessings over the autumn period. If you have an altar in your home, place this jar on the altar.

Supplies
- Jar or container.
- Black salt.
- Pumpkin seeds.
- Rosemary.
- Mugwort.
- Marigold flower.
- Carnelian gemstone.
- Tourmaline gemstone.
- Black candle.

Instructions:
1. Sit in a North-Westerly direction.
2. Place the open jar on the table or surface on which you are working.
3. Lay your ingredients in a circle around the jar with the candle in the 12 o'clock position to the jar.
4. Light the candle.
5. One by one, take your ingredients and place them in the jar.
6. Close the jar and seal it with wax.

Yule Blessing Spell

Yule is a holiday celebrated towards the end of December (the dates vary each year) and is often celebrated alongside Christmas.

Yule is about cycles, birth and rebirth, overcoming challenges, the search for meaning, rest and wisdom.

Create this jar spell at the start of the Yule season and it will bring good fortune and blessings over the winter period and into the new year. If you have an altar in your home, place this jar on the altar.

Supplies
- Jar or container.
- Cinnamon.
- Pinecones.
- Cloves
- Orange peel.
- Rosemary.
- A sprig of evergreen or pine tree.
- Gold candle.

Instructions:
1. Sit in a North facing direction.
2. Place the open jar on the table or surface on which you are working.
3. Lay your ingredients in a circle around the jar with the gold candle in the 12 o'clock position to the jar.
4. Light the candle.
5. One by one, take your ingredients and place them in the jar.
6. Close the jar and seal it with the wax.

Moon Phase Jar Spells

New Moon Spell

The New Moon is a great time to make jar spells related to curses, banishing, divination, love and sex, shadow magic, soul searching and new beginnings.

Supplies
- Jar or container.
- Pen.
- Paper.
- Wormwood.
- Vervain.
- Bird feather.
- Black candle.

Instructions:
1. Write your intention on a slip of paper and add it to the jar.
2. Add the rest of the ingredients.
3. Close the jar and seal with wax.

Waxing Crescent Spell

A waxing crescent moon phase is a great time to make jar spells related to attraction, wealth, success, luck, friendship, binding, and positivity.

Supplies
- Jar or container.
- Pen.
- Paper.
- Wool.
- Angelica.
- Basil.
- Blackberry leaves.
- A green, pink, white or yellow candle.

1. Write your intention on a slip of paper and add it to the jar.
2. Add the rest of the ingredients.
3. Close the jar and seal with wax.

First Quarter Spell

The first quarter moon phase is a great time to make jar spells related to creativity, motivation, divination, strength, growth, and development.

Supplies
- Jar or container.
- Pen.
- Paper.
- Bluebell flowers.
- Honeysuckle.
- Dried grains.
- A gold, green or orange candle.

Instructions:
1. Write your intention on a slip of paper and add it to the jar.
2. Add the rest of the ingredients.
3. Close the jar and seal with wax.

Waxing Gibbous Spell

The waxing gibbous moon phase is a great time to make jar spells related to motivation, growth, good health, and success.

Supplies
- Jar or container.
- Pen.
- Paper.
- Chamomile.
- Ivy.
- Thyme.
- Yarrow.
- An orange, green or purple candle.

Instructions:
1. Write your intention on a slip of paper and add it to the jar.
2. Add the rest of the ingredients.
3. Close the jar and seal with wax.

Full Moon Spell

The full moon is a great time to make jar spells related to love and sex, healing, charging, banishing, cleansing, protection, and completing goals.

Supplies
- Jar or container.
- Pen.
- Paper.
- Cinnamon.
- Clove.
- Pomegranate seeds.
- A red or green candle.

Instructions:
1. Write your intention on a slip of paper and add it to the jar.
2. Add the rest of the ingredients.
3. Close the jar and seal with wax.

Waning Gibbous Spell

The waning gibbous moon phase is a great time to make jar spells related to undoing curses, undoing bindings, relinquishing, and expelling bad energies.

Supplies
- Jar or container.
- Pen.
- Paper.
- Cinnamon.
- Ginger.
- Nettle.
- A white candle.

Instructions:
1. Write your intention on a slip of paper and add it to the jar.
2. Add the rest of the ingredients.
3. Close the jar and seal with wax.

Last Quarter Spell

The last quarter moon phase is a great time to make jar spells related to relinquishing, banishing, and ridding yourself of negative energies.

Supplies
- Jar or container.
- Pen.
- Paper.
- Ginger.
- Ginseng.
- Vanilla.
- A white candle.

Instructions:
1. Write your intention on a slip of paper and add it to the jar.
2. Add the rest of the ingredients.
3. Close the jar and seal with wax.

Waning Crescent Spell

The waning crescent moon phase is a great time to make jar spells related to balance, success, wisdom and atonement.

Supplies
- Jar or container.
- Pen.
- Paper.
- Angelica.
- Basil.
- Sage.
- A green, purple, orange, pink or white candle.

Instructions:
1. Write your intention on a slip of paper and add it to the jar.
2. Add the rest of the ingredients.
3. Close the jar and seal with wax.

Hex Jar Spells

Warning: The following section contains hex jar spells. A hex is a type of spell that is believed to bring bad luck or harm to the person it is cast upon. They differ slightly from curses in that they are short-term, unlike a curse which is long-term. It is important to remember that although hexes are a short lived spell, they can still be intense and harmful.

The ethical issues around hexing are complex. On one hand, many people believe that hexing is morally wrong, as it involves wishing harm upon another person. On the other hand, some argue that hexing or cursing can be seen as a form of self-defence or retribution for harm that has already occurred.

In general, it's considered unethical to harm others through hexing as it goes against the principles of compassion and non-violence. Moreover, it's important to consider the potential consequences of such actions, as they can create further harm and suffering. I suggest looking at other, more positive spells, before deciding on a hex. Hexing should be the last option.

A Traditional Hex Spell

This spell is made with traditional hexing ingredients. For a prolonged effect, bury the jar in the ground. This is considered a medium intensity spell; it won't necessarily harm the recipient but it will teach them a lesson.

Supplies
- Jar or container.
- Cooking oil.
- Black pepper.
- Chilli flakes or cayenne pepper.
- Clove of garlic.
- Rusty nails.
- Square of toilet paper or kitchen roll.
- Pen.

Instructions:
1. Pour oil into your jar.
2. Add the black pepper, chilli flakes/cayenne pepper, the clove of garlic, and the rusty nail.
3. Put the lid on the jar and shake to mix.
4. Take the square of toilet paper or kitchen roll and write the name of the person you wish to hex, nine times.
5. Cross out their name, nine times.
6. Fold the paper three times, making sure to do it away from you.
7. Add the paper to the jar and close the lid.
8. Shake again.

Curse with Kindness Spell

Use this spell when someone has done you wrong, but you don't want to cause long term or serious damage to them.

Supplies
- Jar or container.
- Any of the following; basil, clover, garlic, mugwort, violet, yarrow or wormwood.
- Any of the following gemstones; aventurine, bloodstone, red jasper or rhodonite.
- Slip of paper.

- Pen.
- Black pepper.
- Sugar.

Instructions:
1. Add your herbs/spices to the jar, followed by the gemstones.
2. On the slip of paper, write their name and the following words; "May misery reign until you learn to play nice again."
3. Fold the paper towards you and add it to the jar.
4. Add the sugar to the jar if you haven't already.
5. Close the jar and shake to activate.
6. Shake the jar every time you think this person needs a reminder.

Sour Spell

This jar spell is designed to "sour" someone's life and relationships; it will last as long as you keep the jar sealed. Unlike other hex jar spells that suggest using vinegar, vinegar should not be added to this jar. It will strip the rust from the nails and therefore affect the potency of the spell. This is considered a potent and strong spell, and as such, please consider carefully if this is what you want for the recipient. Should you wish to reverse this spell, you may need the help of a more experienced practitioner.

Supplies
- Jar or container.
- A sample of your own waste, such as urine.
- Shards of glass.
- Dead wasps.
- Rusted nails.
- Thorns.
- Water collected in a storm.

Instructions:
1. Do not cleanse any of your ingredients or jar.
2. Add your ingredients to the jar and seal.
3. Periodically open the jar to "burp" it; i.e. let out the gases caused by the rust and decomposition. Otherwise you risk the gases expanding and shattering the jar.

Stop A Gossip Spell

Use this jar spell when someone is talking about you behind your back or spreading malicious words about you. It won't "hurt" the person as such, but it will make them stop their gossip.

Supplies
- Jar or container.
- Something sharp such as glass, a nail, or a razor.
- Soil.
- Black pepper.
- Salt.
- Pen.
- Paper.
- Black candle.

Instructions:
1. Write the name of the person on a slip of paper. If it is not safe to use their name, use a code or initials.
2. Fold the paper away from you and put it in the jar.
3. Add the ingredients to the jar.
4. Close the jar and seal with wax.

Pay Back Spell

Use this jar spell when someone has wronged you. This is considered a very powerful piece of folk magic, so please use it with caution. Reversing a spell like this is difficult and may require help from a more power practitioner.

Supplies
- Jar or container bigger enough to fit a chilli pepper inside.
- Paper.
- Pen.
- A fresh hot chilli pepper.
- Nine pins or sewing needles.
- Black candle.

Instructions:

1. Write the name of the person on a slip of paper. If it is not safe to use their name, use a code or initials.
2. Roll or fold the paper.
3. Using three pins, pin the paper to the chilli pepper.
4. The other six pins should be stuck into the chilli pepper directly.
5. Add the chilli with the paper and pins to the jar.
6. Close the jar and seal with wax.

Thievery Spell

Use this jar spell when someone has "stolen" something from you; this could be a literal theft or something metaphorical such as stolen your time, stolen the best years of your life, stolen a lover, stolen a friend, or stolen your innocence.

Supplies

- Jar or container.
- Paper.
- Pen.
- Apple cider vinegar.
- One clove of garlic.
- Black pepper.
- Coriander.
- Wormwood.
- Chilli flakes.

Instructions:

1. Write the name of the person on a slip of paper. Use a code or initials if it's not safe to use their name.
2. Fold the paper as small as you can and add it to the jar.
3. Add the apple cider vinegar, garlic, black pepper, coriander, wormwood and chilli flakes.
4. Close the jar.
5. Let the jar sit for four days, shaking once each day.
6. After the four days, throw the ingredients away and dispose of the jar.

Thanks for reading my book
and supporting me,
I appreciate it.

If you liked this book
and found it useful,
let me know your opinion
by leaving a short review
on Amazon.

Download your BONUS.

A blank spellbook to fill with your best spells

Scan the code below to download your BONUS

Printed in Great Britain
by Amazon

32830481R00059